The Book of
Energy Leadership Frameworks

By Jimmy Y. Jia

First Published 2017
Seattle, WA 98122

The Book of Energy Leadership Frameworks
By Jimmy Y. Jia

Front cover, back cover, and illustrations by Karina Zikan

ISBN: 1548465429
ISBN-13: 978-1548465421

This book is dedicated to the students of the Bainbridge Graduate Institute,
Pinchot University, and Presidio Graduate School,
especially those who took my course in sustainable energy.

Through your curiosity we studied, questioned, and co-created
many frameworks for wiser approaches to energy problems.

Special thanks to Grace Carlson, Chad Evans, and Judy Stein
for your diligent edits.

Thank you for letting me take the class with you.

Table of Contents

Introduction: Why This Book?

The two hardest parts of problem solving:

    (1) How to start,

        and

    (2) When to stop.

Gathering information for a framework is a very good place to start. System boundaries offer a place to stop because there's nothing left to explore. Where one draws the boundary determines the possible set of solutions. Knowing that a problem is solvable is half the battle.

Every system has internal and external properties. On the inside are *processes*. On the outside are *inputs* and *outputs*. Anything excluded from consideration is part of the *environment* (or context).

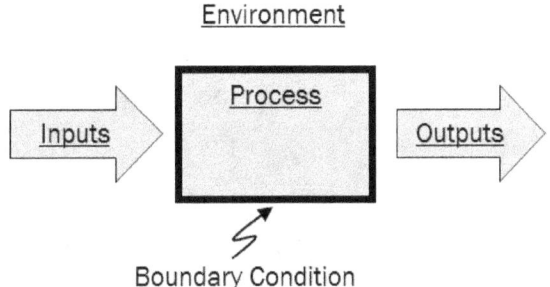

Some boundaries are movable, some are not. The **CONSERVATION OF ENERGY**, the most fundamental of systems, has immovable boundaries since it's based on the laws of physics. Other boundaries, such as those in **THE ENERGY LITERACY MATRIX**, are designed to be expanded by the user.

Performance improvements happen inside the boundaries. Leaders can find more efficient use of resources and achieve better productivity. These frameworks are a form of decision support that help leaders organize data into manageable options.

Innovations happen at the boundaries, for that is where ideas not currently inside the system emerge. When innovation occurs, it creates *new systems* that redefines the boundaries. Understanding system boundaries of frameworks help shift paradigms of business practices, creating competitive advantage.

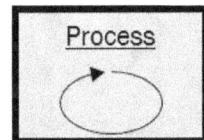

Innovations that optimizes processes *inside* your boundary

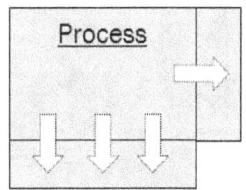

Innovations that integrate ideas *outside* your boundary

How to use this book

This book is meant to be a cursory overview of tools available to leaders who need to make strategic decisions on energy management. Each framework is accompanied with a brief explanation and some examples of applications. The reader is encouraged to do their own research on the frameworks to gain further familiarity and understanding.

Apply these frameworks to problems at hand and solutions may reveal themselves.

1) Select a framework

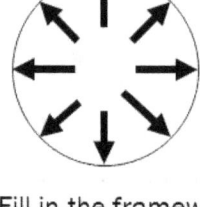

2) Fill in the framework

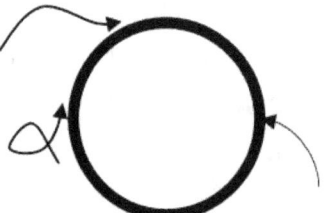

3) Investigate system boundaries

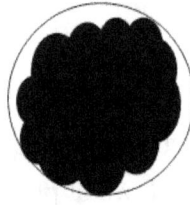

4) Compare actual boundaries to perceived boundaries

5) Innovate at the edges of the system boundaries

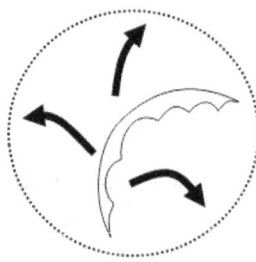

6) Re-center to the new framework, creating a new sector.

Part 1: System Fundamentals

Energy Literacy

Energy enables comfort, convenience and enhances the quality of life.

Managing energy requires an understanding of the technology and the social problem/s being addressed.

These frameworks will help the reader evaluate whether a solution will help them achieve a desired outcome.

The Conservation of Energy

The laws of thermodynamics govern how energy works. Energy cannot be created nor destroyed. The energy system is always in balance and any changes will merely shift the energy. Furthermore, any energy transformation will produce waste. Formally, the equation is:

Energy In = Useful Energy Out + Wasted Energy Out

What it's good for: The diagram for energy balance is a great reminder that energy is a supply chain. *Energy In* encompasses the fuel (coal, natural gas, solar, nuclear, etc.). Energy efficiency and better equipment technologies (LEDs, insulation, etc.) are about the *Transformation*. Acid rain, pollution, and carbon issues are examples of *Wasted Energy Out*. Rarely do we talk about why we consumed the energy in the first place: the value proposition of *Useful Energy Out*. These value propositions include improving comfort, convenience, and the quality of life.

How I use it: I use this framework to quickly categorize conversations, media stories, and technologies I'm asked to evaluate. A common challenge in the cleantech sector is navigating through the complexity of interdependencies between solar companies, carbon sequestration, engine improvements, reforestation, etc. Knowing the category relationships of the conversation helps me understand the applicable market dynamics.

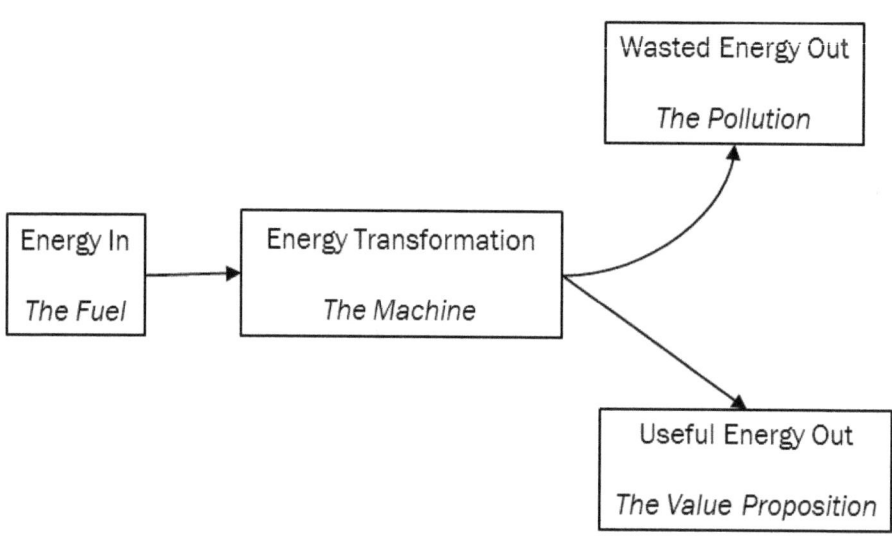

Reference:
Jia J. and Crabtree J. (2015) *Driven by demand: how energy gets its power*, Cambridge UP, Cambridge, United Kingdom.

Energy Flowcharts

Sankey diagrams are a snapshot in time depicting how resources flow from supply to demand. This one is a popular elaboration on THE CONSERVATION OF ENERGY diagram, demonstrating the USA's energy flow.

What it's good for: These charts demonstrate that energy is a supply chain. They reveal the relationship between a resource and how it's used. Note that the source of energy is not always geographically next to where it is consumed.

- Each BOX is a separate industrial sector, with different regulatory regimes, financing mechanisms and rate of returns.
- Each LINE represents a road, transmission line, pipeline, or means of transportation. It shows how the fuel gets to where it's needed.

How I use it: I use it to understand system constraints, choke points, and weaknesses. Supply needs to flow to demand. Geographically, supply may be far away from the demand in which case there needs to be transportation infrastructure in between. It helps determine which business, business model, regulator, or financial constraints exist for a solution.

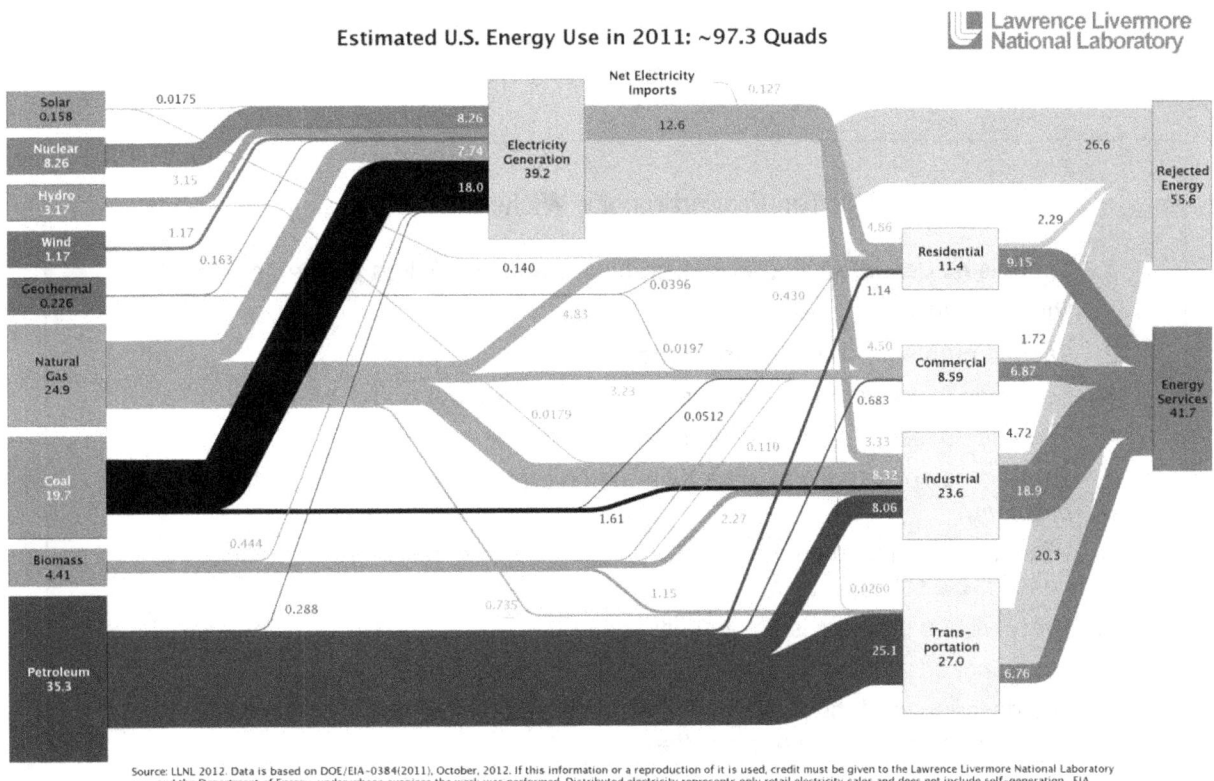

Reference:

Energy flow charts. Lawrence Livermore National Laboratory http://flowcharts.llnl.gov/

The Wicked Problem

A Wicked Problem describes a set of problems that is impossible to solve because of incomplete and contradictory information with constantly shifting requirements. A Tame Problem, such as chess, ceases to exist once a solution is reached since there are no rules governing how to play after a checkmate.

The ten properties of a Wicked Problem are listed below. Energy is a classical wicked problem and property #9 informs us that solutions are frame-of-reference dependent. For instance, "improving the electric grid's carbon efficiency" could be achieved with 100% nuclear plants, 100% distributed solar to reduce transmission losses, or 100% off-grid housing. Each one of these solutions are valid yet imply a different framing of the assumptions and constraints.

What it's good for: Wicked problems need to be *managed*, not *solved*. Addressing a wicked problem requires a strong leader, a strategic goal, and an incremental approach (See THE SCIENCE OF MUDDLING THROUGH).

How I use it: I use this framework to search for underlying assumptions and the frame-of-reference of a solution. Identifying these assumptions can reveal opportunities not considered before.

The Ten Properties of a Wicked Problem

1. There is **no definition** of a wicked problem (defining wicked problems is itself a wicked problem).
2. Wicked problems **do not 'stop'** being problems.
3. Solutions to wicked problems are not true-or-false, but **better-or-worse.**
4. There is **no test of a solution** to a wicked problem.
5. There is no opportunity to learn by trial and error. **Every solution changes the problem.**
6. Wicked problems do not have a describable set of potential solutions nor describable set of actions.
7. Every wicked problem is essentially **unique.**
8. Every wicked problem is a symptom of another problem.
9. The description of the problem is through a **frame of reference**. Any proposed solution only meets the **need of that frame.**
10. Planners are liable for the consequences of the actions they generate [**There will always be unintended consequences**]

Reference:

Rittel, H. and Webber, M. (1973) *Dilemmas in a general theory of planning*, Policy Sciences **4** 155-169

The Clumsy Solution

The Clumsy Solution is an approach to **WICKED PROBLEMS** that categorizes solutions as hierarchical, competitive, or egalitarian.

- *Hierarchical* – using processes and rules to create the pathway for an outcome (such as government regulations that require public commenting before passing judgment).
- *Competitive* – finding the 'best' solution using competitive mechanisms (such as businesses that compete for market share).
- *Egalitarian* – advocating for socially good and ideal solutions (such as public advocacy groups and non-profits that represent environmental causes).

Practically speaking, solutions are some combination of all three with different weightings.

What it's good for: It helps determine whether an industry is in balance. An out-of-balance system exhibits a lot of side effects. For instance, stringent government regulation of utilities has kept prices low. It also hampers innovation (competitive approaches) and raises the bar for renewable integrations (egalitarian approaches).

How I use it: I use this model to find opportunities to bring a sector back into balance. For instance, a solar business which may tap into an individual's environmental concern is a competitive-egalitarian approach that can be a counterbalance to a utility regulatory system.

HIERARCHICAL
(i.e. Government)

COMPETITIVE   **EGALITARIAN**
(i.e. Business)   *(i.e. Advocacy Groups)*

Reference:

Rayner, S. (1995) *A conceptual map of human values for climate change decision making*, in: A. Katama (ed.) *Equity and social considerations related to climate change*. ICIPE Science Press, Nairobi, Kenya

The Energy Literacy Matrix

The Energy Literacy Matrix facilitates a leader's quick understanding of both the technical and social context of any energy resource situation. It combines **THE CONSERVATION OF ENERGY** and **THE CLUMSY SOLUTION**.

An example: incentivizing a large solar farm in the desert could be a viable non-carbon *generation* approach for *government*. However, advocating for using rooftop solar to reduce transmission losses is an *egalitarian/transport* issue, involving a different set of stakeholders.

This framework is also extendable. Adding a time axis enables the discussion of historical issues, present-day concerns, and future opportunities in a sector. Adding fuel extraction before *Generation* or adding pollution after *Consumption* creates a more comprehensive supply chain. This framework can be applied to other supply chains, such as water, agriculture, and minerals.

What it's good for: Leaders can use this framework to grasp the context for any proposed solution. Each box has a different set of companies, regulations, value propositions, and challenges they face. The matrix indicates what the implications and constraints might be for any solution.

How I use it: In addition to using it to understand context, I also use this to make sure that my courses, lectures, and talks are well balanced and comprehensive on any topic.

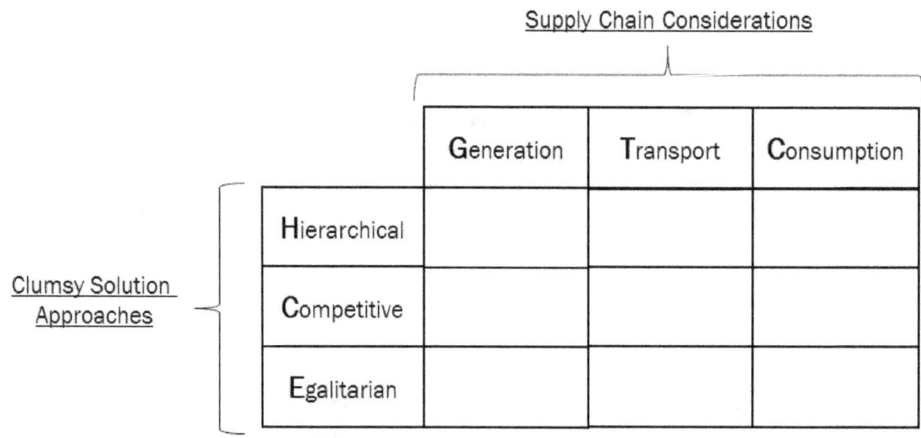

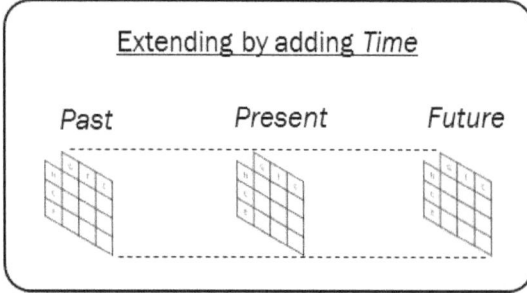

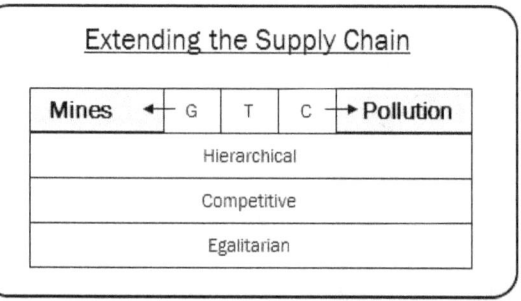

Financial Literacy

A business sustains itself when revenue equals expenses and grows if revenues exceed expenses.

Financial statements are about definitions and categories. They help a leader understand and set strategy, positioning, and evaluate the viability of an organization.

This section is a review of how to use the three main financial statements for decision support.

Balance Sheet

A balance sheet is a snapshot in time of what an organization owns or owes. The two sides must always be equal and are governed by the equation:

Assets = Liabilities + Shareholder Equity

- *Assets* – a list of what an organization has, such as cash, equipment, and goodwill.
- *Liabilities* – items that must be paid: bills, payroll, loans, and others.
- *Shareholder's Equity* – what's left over once all bills are paid. This is split amongst the owners and shareholders of the company, in the form of dividends.

Double entry bookkeeping is a system that requires at least two accounting entries per each transaction, once for assets and once for liabilities.

Balance sheets can be optimized to "look good". For instance, an energy savings performance contract (ESPC) is an *off-balance sheet* financing mechanism because the company is purchasing the services of the equipment instead of buying the equipment itself. This can give the company flexibility to execute on projects. Relying too much on off-balance sheet methods can create large problems (i.e., Enron).

What it's good for: The balance sheet shows the status of the company: what assets to use to turn into revenue or what liability constraints need to be satisfied.

How I use it: Simplistically, I use the balance sheet to figure out what's available "to play" with.

Assets	Liabilities
What the company owns	What the company owes
	Owner's Equity
	What's left over for you and your investors

Income Statement (Profit & Loss or P&L)

An income statement shows the *activities* between two balance sheets. It shows where money came from (*revenue*) and how it was spent (*expenses*). Any expenses not related to company operations, such as interest, taxes, depreciation, and amortization are considered *Non-Operating Expenses*.

Gross Profit, *EBITDA* (earnings before interest, tax, depreciation, and amortization) and *Net Earnings* are the key metrics in a P&L.

The P&L is a financial version of a strategy document. Activities should be funded based on company priorities. For instance, a company may decide to invest in marketing to boost sales, or focus on equipment to increase production. The P&L should support the stated business plan.

What it's good for: An investor will use the historical P&L to understand a company's strategy. An entrepreneur uses the future P&L (aka *financial pro forma*) to forecast the earnings potential of their business.

How I use it: As an entrepreneur, I use the P&L mostly as a pro forma to forecast future earning potential.

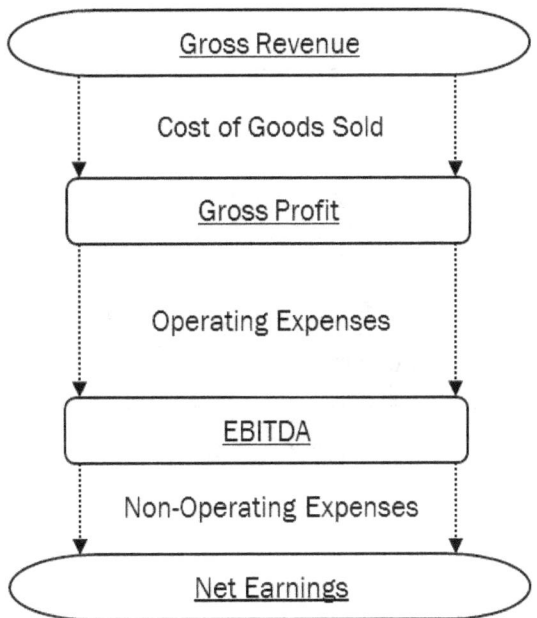

Cash Flow Statement

A cash flow statement shows the exchange of *cash* between two balance sheets. Cash from operating activities are recorded in the **INCOME STATEMENT**. Investment returns, such as those from real estate or financing activities (i.e., cash investment from a venture capital firm) are considered non-cash activities.

The cash flow statement reconciles the difference between operating activities and the bank account. Not every financial activity recorded in the **INCOME STATEMENT** generates immediate cash. For instance, a utility bill received today that is due next month will not affect cash flow today. Likewise, a client contract signed today for $1,000 but paid upon delivery in 3 months also does not affect the cash today.

What it's good for: Cash is king. Without cash, a company goes bankrupt, even if it has a lot of valuable assets. The *free cash flow* model can also be used to determine the enterprise value of a company (DCF, or Discounted Cash Flow is one such method to determine enterprise value).

How I use it: Making sure I can make payroll or have the funds to invest in the next new idea!

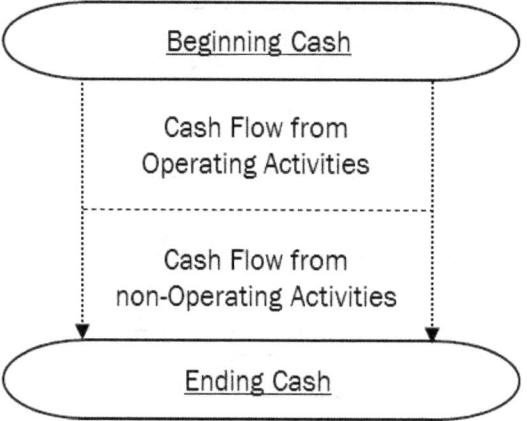

Decision Support of Financial Activities

The three financial statements represent the financial health of an organization. It helps the decision makers answer these basic questions:

- Where was I / Where am I / Where do I want to be? → **BALANCE SHEET**
- What did I do / What am I planning to do? → **INCOME STATEMENT**
- How much did we spend / Do I have the money to get there? → **CASH FLOW STATEMENT**

What it's good for: Based on these three statements, one can tell a lot about the path a company took, what decisions they made and where they are going. Statements in the future are called "pro forma".

How I use it: I use this to remind myself what financial statement I need to ask for based on what question I'm trying to answer. Any question to do with operations goes to the **INCOME STATEMENT**. Any question to do with current state analysis goes to the **BALANCE SHEET**. Any questions on how risky a company can afford to be goes to the **CASH FLOW STATEMENT**.

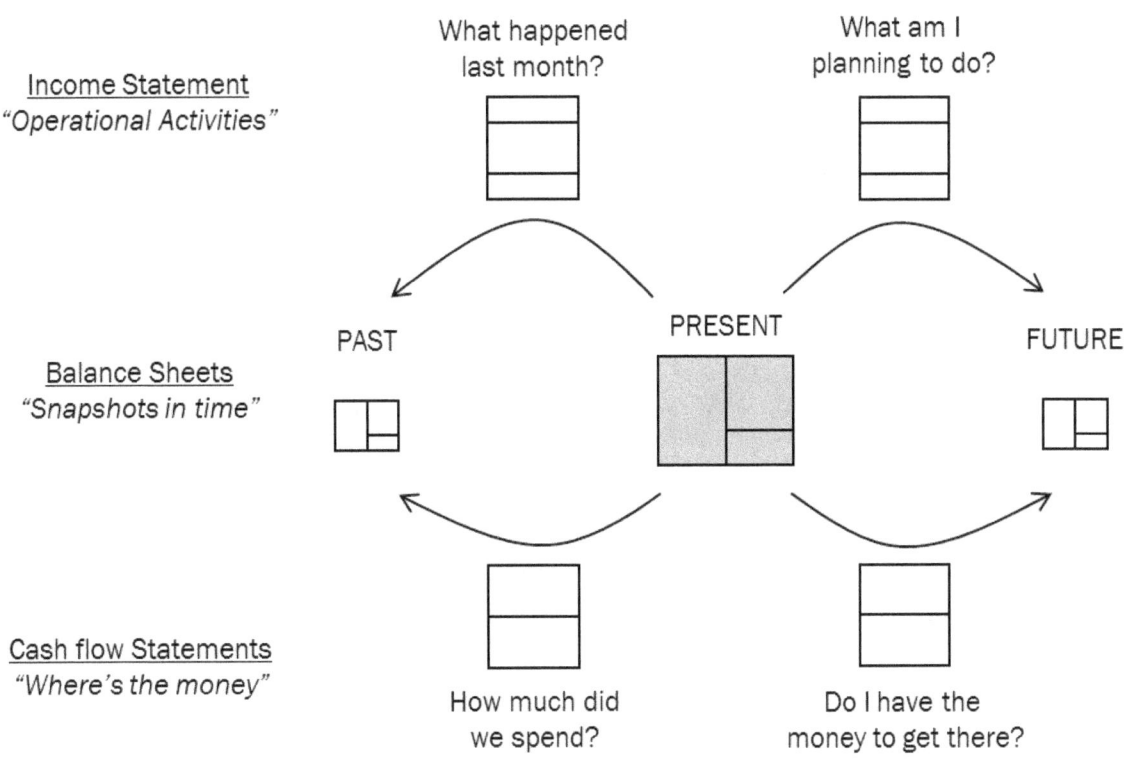

Carbon Management Frameworks

Carbon is generated as a direct outcome of consuming energy.

Energy flows are directly correlated with operational activity.

Operations are funded by budget plans and cash.

Therefore, financial decisions that improve operational efficiencies will have a direct effect on a company's carbon footprint.

These tools leverage financial tools for positive carbon outcomes.

The Utility Line-Item

The true cost of utilities is far greater than just bills. The Utility Line-Item documents the company's internal and external factors that are directly or indirectly affected by resource consumption.

- *Utility Assets and Expenses* – include both physical and operational costs. *Utility bills* are frequently the only expense a leader will consider when making an energy decision. Yet, as this diagram shows, utility resources and their uses are pervasive across the entire organization.
- *Utility Opportunities* – include delivering on customer promises while using fewer resources. Higher resource efficiency increases profitability, reduces risks, and increases competitive advantage in a rapidly changing market.
- *Utility Risks* – factors that prevent a company to deliver on their customer promise. Energy risks include rate increases, loss of key facilities personnel, or equipment downtime.

What it's good for: The line-item is a *snapshot in time* of a company's utility assets, opportunities, and risks. This diagram is the energy analogy of the BALANCE SHEET.

How I use it: When I start working with a client, I use this as a tool to diagnose the true cost of utilities. This budget can be as high as 10% of a company's operating expenses. Since energy consumption and carbon footprint are intimately intertwined, this analysis also exposes a company's carbon risk exposure, an often-overlooked and underappreciated factor.

	Internal Factors	External Factors
Assets and Expenses	• Team & expertise • Equipment • Recurring maintenance • Facility operations • Equipment upgrades / retrofits • Cost of Capital: reserve funds	• Utility bills (electricity, water, natural gas, trash, diesel, etc.) • Contractors • Landlord, tenants, competitors • Equipment availability • Cost of Capital: incentives, loans
Opportunities	• Improved profitability • Increased resiliency • Accelerate value creation	• New technologies • New financing • Market conditions
Risks	• Equipment downtime • Staff turnover • Changing customer requirements • Lost productivity	• Rate increases • Policy changes • Carbon pricing • Blackouts and brownouts • Buys a "greenwashed" solution

For More Information:

Bloomberg, M, et. al. (2016) *Recommendations of the task force on climate-related financial disclosures.*

De-Carbonization Workflow

De-carbonizing an organization is a form of change management that needs to evolve at the pace of the organization. Here are some industry best practices that reduce carbon exposure and risk.

- *Set a strategic vision* – Align internal stakeholders on the strategic goal. Energy and utilities affect the entire organization and require multi-functional and departmental representation.
- *Gain certainty over assets* – Consolidate the **UTILITY LINE-ITEM** and the responsibility of the line-item to a single person or department.
- *Mitigate risk* – Take actionable steps based on the **CARBON RESOURCE PRIORITIZATION** to reduce consumption and carbon exposure.
- *Innovate solutions* – Uncover new and better ways to accomplish the same tasks. It is common for innovative solutions to surface while implementing ideas.
- *Increase productivity* – A lower carbon exposure increases an organization's competitive advantage, enabling higher levels of productivity.

What it's good for: This workflow depicts tangible steps that can be taken to improve an organization, regardless of the maturity of their carbon management system.

How I use it: I use this to determine what activities and tasks to recommend based on their existing practices.

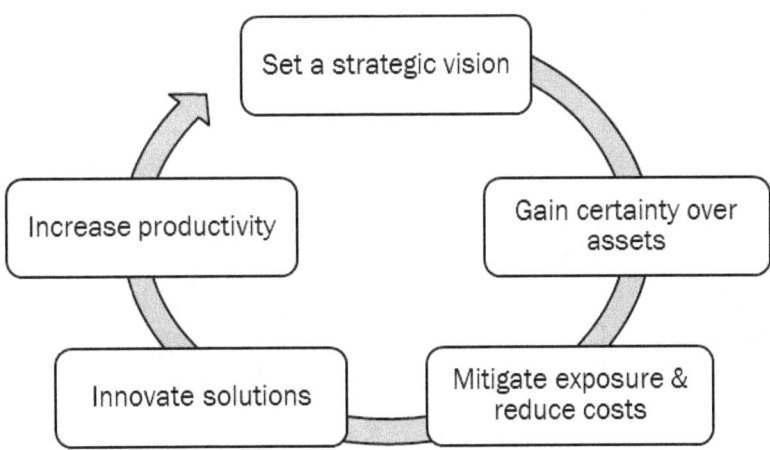

Decision Support of Energy Activities

Energy and cash both flow through an organization. We can therefore adopt the tools used to manage financial flows to manage energy flows. Fundamentally, the CONSERVATION OF ENERGY and double-entry accounting of the BALANCE SHEET is the connection between energy and finance. Both systems *must* stay in balance.

$$\text{Energy In} = \text{Wasted Energy Out} + \text{Useful Energy Out}$$
$$\text{Assets} = \text{Liabilities} + \text{Shareholder's Equity}$$

- The UTILITY LINE-ITEM is a snapshot in time of the energy assets, opportunities, and risks.
- The DE-CARBONIZATION WORKFLOW represents the activities that change over time.
- Consumption metrics are key performance indicators that monitor consumption: kWh, therms, gallons, and BTUs. This is the category where utility bills reside.

What it's good for: This framework connects the leading indicators of future plans to the lagging indicators of past consumption. *What* consumes energy, such as equipment and people. *How* one consumes energy includes operating hours and production cycles. *Why* one consumes energy includes keeping employees comfortable and meeting customer service requirements.

How I use it: I use this to help organize information into digestible chunks. Different stakeholders in an organization are responsible for different sets of data, implementation, and funding.

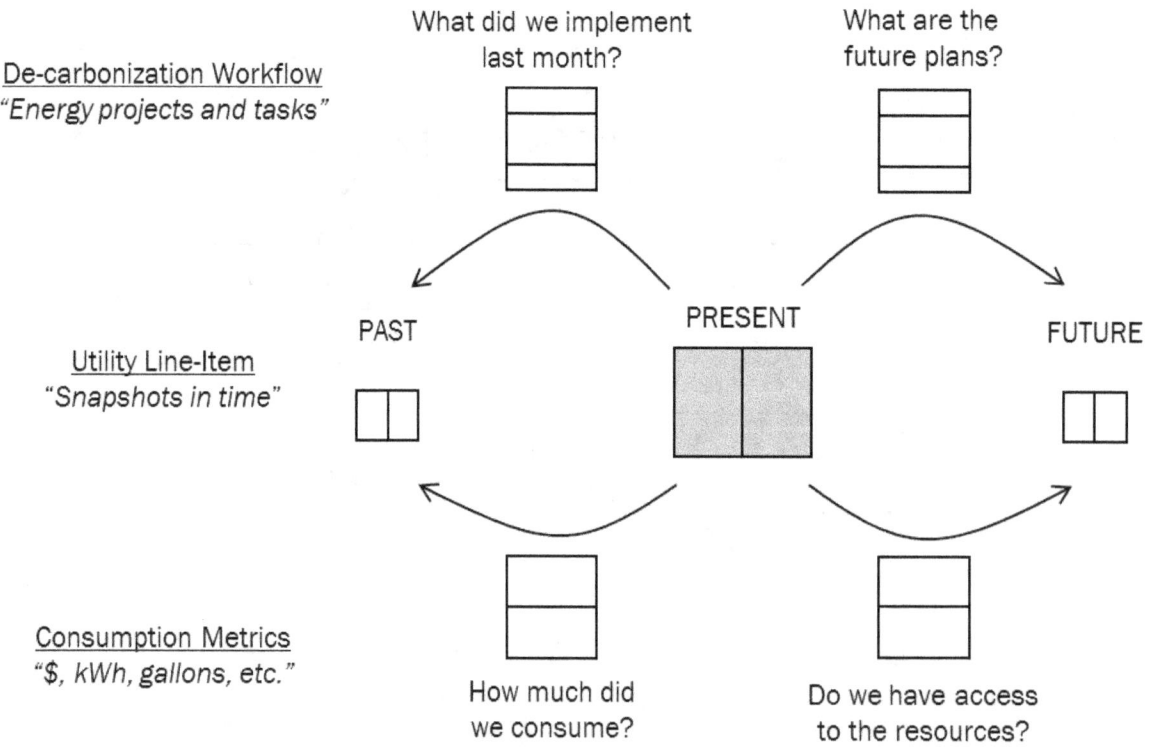

Waste Resource Prioritization

Starting from the early 1990s, Germany adopted a waste resource framework that has successfully reduced landfills to less than 0.5% of municipal solid waste (U.S. landfills represent more than 50%). Key to this success was declaring landfills a negative externality and repositioning the entire waste management sector to minimize them. Success came from prioritizing activities to maximize economic value of the resource before burying it underground.

- *Waste Prevention* – Strategies that include *avoidance* (only use what one needs), *source reduction* (build it to last) and *reuse* (use it more than once).
- *Waste Minimization* – Strategies such as *quality improvements* (upcycle the product once its lifespan is over), *recycle* (if it can't be upcycled, then recycle it) and *waste-to-energy* (extract the embodied energy from the material to run the grid).
- *Waste Disposal* – Strategies to be pursued one call other approaches have been exhausted. These include *incineration* (purely for volume reduction purposes) and *landfilling* (burying the trash)

What it's good for: This framework has been so successful at extracting value that the German resource management sector is a €50 billion industry, much larger than the landfill sector itself. It demonstrated how to extract additional value from the resource supply chain.

How I use it: I use this framework to analyze and optimize a company's materials resource supply chain. I've also extended this to the **CARBON RESOURCE PRIORITIZATION**.

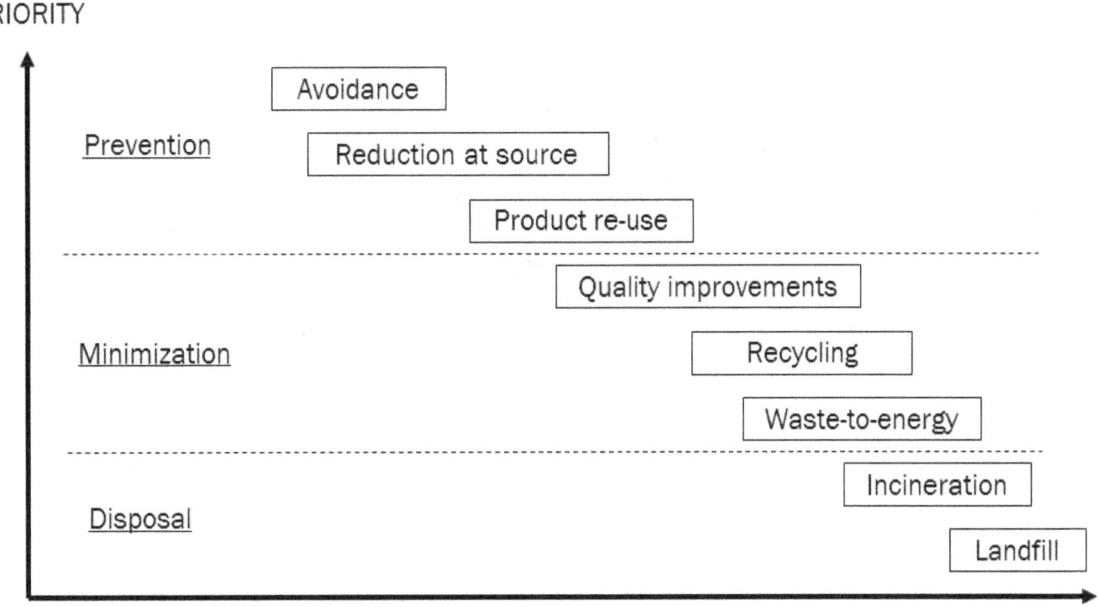

Reference:

Jia J. and Crabtree J. (2015) *Driven by demand: how energy gets its power*, Cambridge UP, Cambridge, United Kingdom.

Carbon Resource Prioritization

Carbon is a negative resource that can be minimized using analogous principles to the WASTE RESOURCE PRIORITIZATION. This can be accomplished by focusing on outcomes that minimize carbon and maximize economic value.

- *Carbon Prevention* – achieving outcomes without consuming any carbon. *Land use planning* for high-density, mixed use neighborhoods eliminates the need for transportation carbon. *Passive housing* reduces the energy needs for heating and cooling.
- *Carbon Minimization* – consuming the least amount necessary. This includes *energy efficiency* and reusing *waste heat* for additional purposes. Consume *non-carbon power* sources first, such as those from solar and wind.
- *Carbon Management* – for activities that require fossil fuel generation (i.e., backup power, off-grid applications). Implement *co-generation* facilities first to reuse heat, and use *clean fuels* next if co-generation is not an option. *Carbon sequestration*, which removes carbon from the air, is a technology that cleans up the carbon messes already created. These should be pursued last.

What it's good for: This brings together and prioritizes seemingly disparate technologies (from urban planning to salt caverns for CO_2 sequestration) in a holistic framework.

How I use it: I use this to prioritize decisions that a company could make to reduce its carbon footprint. I've applied this model to decarbonize operations, a product line, or for the development of new decarbonized product/s.

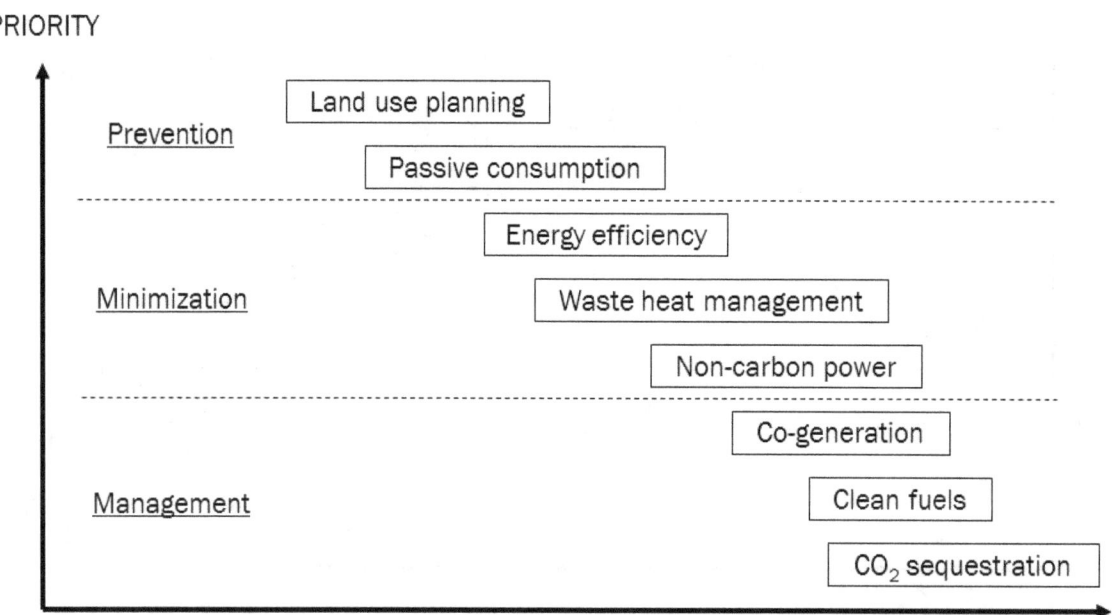

System Boundaries

Knowing what's at a system's boundaries helps eliminate impractical ideas and reveal where innovations can take place.

Energy equations describe system boundaries that cannot be shifted.

Understanding the properties of variance can help a leader decide between managing for risk or managing for innovation.

Kaizen: Innovations that Improve Processes

Kaizen, a method for continuous process improvements, is a way to identify and implement innovations inside system boundaries. It is a daily process, enabling individuals to make controlled experiments to improve their effectiveness. Although each improvement is small and incremental, in aggregate, they can dramatically improve productivity and reduce waste.

There are two continuous cycles of analysis to help teams identify and reduce waste. The first cycle involves root-cause analysis (*Plan, Do, Check, Act*) to address fundamental issues rather than symptomatic ones. The second cycle is an example of subset-processes. This one connects the implementation of a solution (*Do*) to determining if it solved the problem (*Check*).

What it's good for: Kaizen is a great process improvement technique that decreases variances in manufacturing and business processes. This results in higher efficiencies.

How I use it: I use this method to streamline existing processes and improve efficiency.

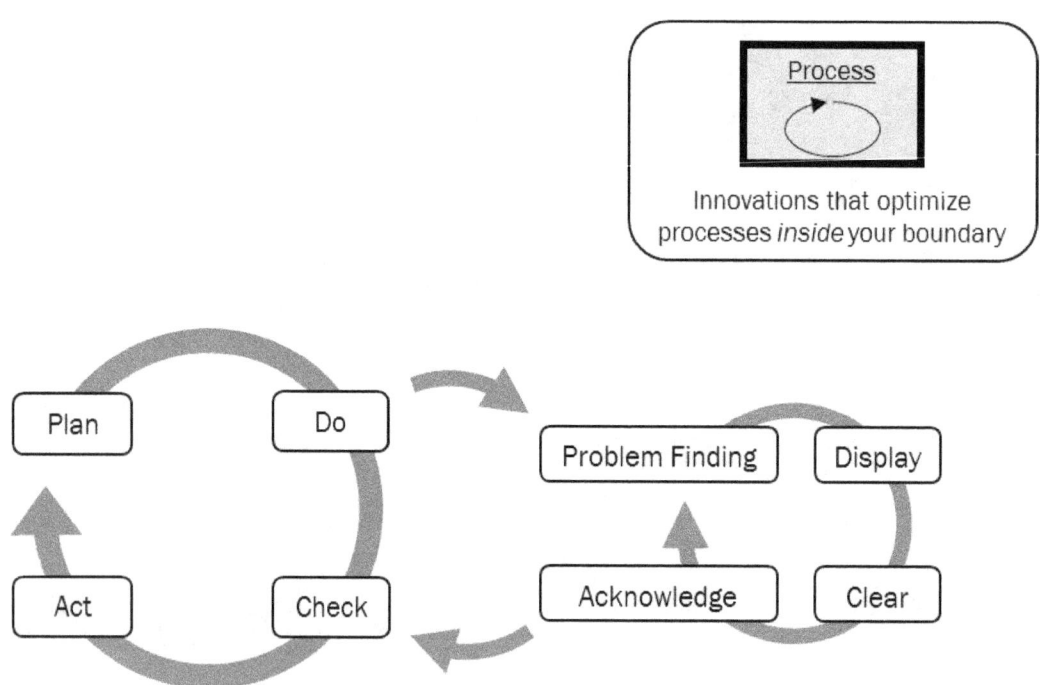

Disruptions: Innovations at the Intersection of Infrastructure

Combining two existing ideas is a method of redefining the system boundaries. More often than we care to admit, our problems have already been solved in a different sector. Revolutionary innovations usually begin as the innocent merging of two seemingly disparate ideas.

For example, the evolution of a wooden tramways to the iron railways is an innovation internal to the transportation sector. It increased the efficiency of horse-drawn caravans. Likewise, James Watt's steam pump miniaturized the state-of-the-art technology to improve the removal of water from coal mines. It turns out that Watt's steam pump was small enough to put on an iron railway, thus creating the rail travel industry. The electric grid was created when a stationary steam engine enabled electric generation to run a light bulb. This pattern exists in all fields, including chefs who re-invent classic dishes into their own signature variations.

What it's good for: Innovative ideas are inspired from different sources. Artists know they need stimulation to be creative. Scientists frequently investigate "how nature solved this problem" when applying it to their own work.

How I use it: When I'm looking for 'out of the box' solutions, I usually examine a different system with similar properties. The lessons learned elsewhere may apply to my current situation.

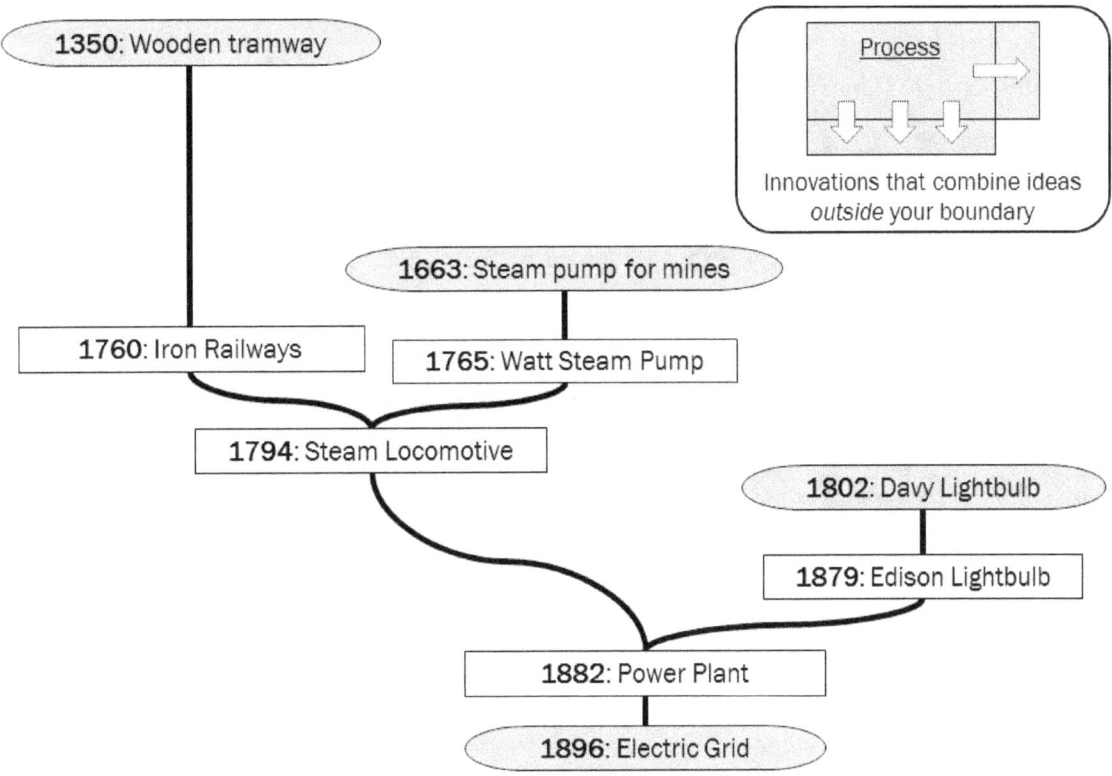

Reference:

Marine Agogue, Armand Hatchuel. *Reinventing classics: the hidden design strategies of renowned chefs* Res Eng Design (2016) **27** 165

Transportation Boundaries: Kinetic Energy

The Kinetic Energy equation governs the boundary condition of the transportation sector. At first glance, most of these attributes are fairly apparent. A heavier object needs more energy to move than a lighter object (a motorcycle uses less gasoline than minivan). The further the distance, the more energy required. Trains are more energy efficient than automobiles because rails have less resistance than paved roads.

What it's good for: The model reveals the market dynamics of the transportation sector. Government policy drives decisions on the *resistance* variable. The USA's transportation policy is to build highways while Japan's transportation policy is to build rail. Individual choice affects the *mass* variable as individuals decide whether to buy an SUV or a bicycle. Premium transportation services modify the *distance* and *time* variables. In expensive city centers, people may walk to work and not own a car at all. Many states allow single drivers to pay a fee to drive in less congested High Occupancy Vehicle (HOV) lanes that are normally excluded to them.

How I use it: It helps me understand what problem is being solved in the transportation sector. For example, Lyft and Uber claim to reduce the number of cars (*mass*) and increase convenience (*time*).

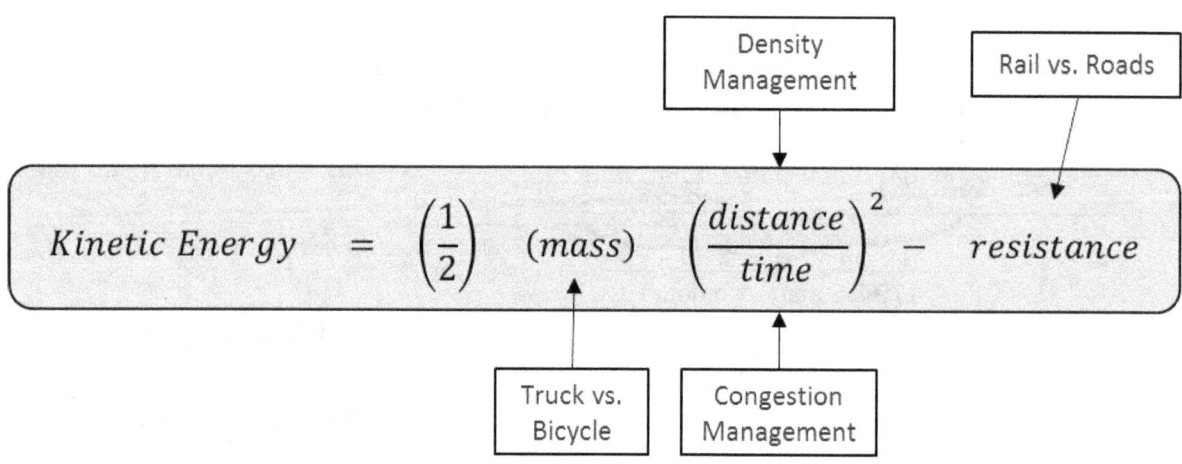

$$Kinetic\ Energy \;=\; \left(\frac{1}{2}\right)\ (mass)\ \left(\frac{distance}{time}\right)^{2} \;-\; resistance$$

Refrigeration Boundaries: The Ideal Gas Law

The Ideal Gas Law dictates how technology that uses gases work, including refrigeration, air conditioning and internal combustion engines. Refrigeration and air conditioning reduce *temperature* by cleverly manipulating the *pressure* and *volume* of the system. Internal combustion engines use rapid increases in *volume* to drive pistons by carefully managing the *temperature* and *pressure* inside the cylinder.

NOTE: This equation does not describe energy required – only how the actions happens. For energy, please see HEATING AND COOLING BOUNDARIES: THE ENTHALPY EQUATION.

What it's good for: This describes refrigeration technologies and explains why hotter gasses cause more damaging explosions. NOTE: Some cooling techniques, such as Peltier cooling, do not use gasses and therefore this equation does not apply.

How I use it: When someone tries to explain an innovation in refrigeration, I use this model to understand how their technology works and to understand what their innovation tries to improve.

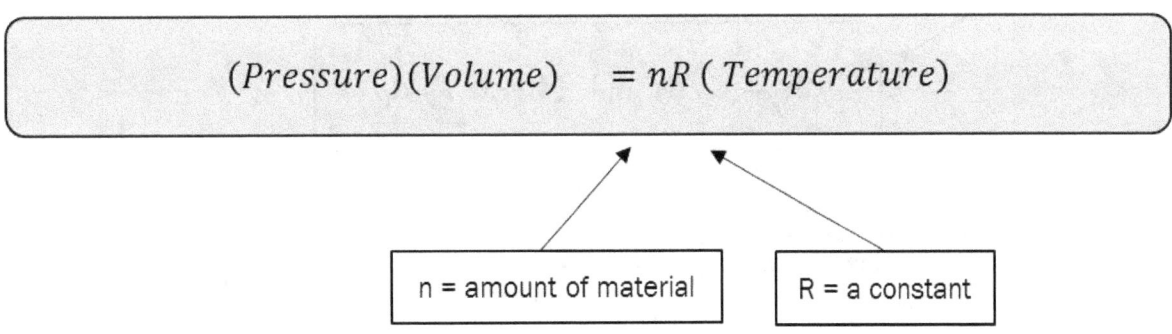

$$(Pressure)(Volume) = nR\,(Temperature)$$

n = amount of material

R = a constant

Heating and Cooling Boundaries: The Enthalpy Equation

Enthalpy is the measure of the total heat content of a system. This equation depicts how heating and cooling works in any situation (The **IDEAL GAS LAW** equation only applies to gasses). It also shows why heat management is complicated!

First, there's a lot of calculus. The "d's", which represent derivatives, shows that *changing* temperature and *changing* pressure affects *changes* in enthalpy. The implication: heat is a comparative measure against a reference point. Indeed, one does not "have heat". One "has more heat than something else". The reference point is frequently implied and unstated. For instance, *generating heat* implies creating more heat than the surroundings (the reference point). *Feeling warm* implies that one's body temperature is higher than one's comfort preference (the reference point).

What it's good for: This is a complete model for any analysis of heat. However, it's usually too complicated for a leader to use directly.

How I use it: I use this model to understand an innovation's implied or unstated reference points. The reference points create the context and boundary of the system.

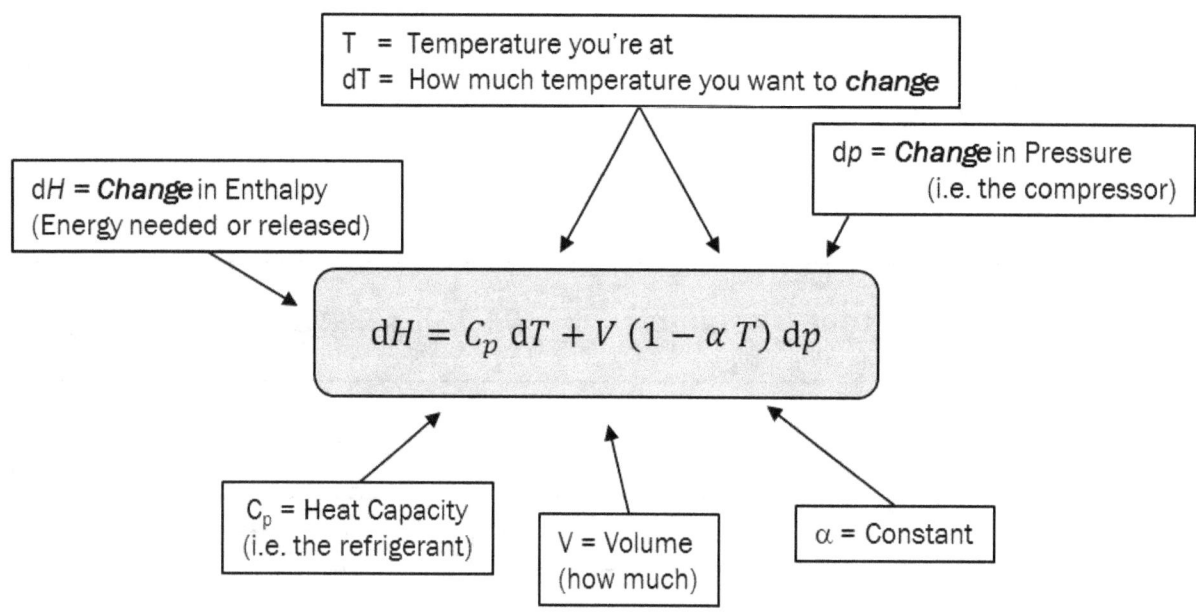

The Context of Results: Average vs. Variance

Usually when we make a change to a system, we intend to change the average – or the results. Frequently we overlook that we also change the variance – or the context of the system. The two can be hard to tease apart.

For example, most people consider climate change to imply an increase in *average* global temperatures. Climate change is also increasing the *variance* of global temperature – hence more extreme cold and extreme heat events. Climate skeptics frequently point to extreme cold events as evidence that the average temperature has not substantially changed.

This is the challenge that **WICKED PROBLEMS** face – both the average (results) and the variance (context) is changed through applying a solution. Unfortunately, most standard statistical techniques assume that variance stays the same before and after implementing a solution. In fact, linear regressions require *homoscedasticity* – or that the variance of data in groups is the same.

What it's good for: Most innovations are pitched as changing the average. Understanding how they also change the variance helps to understand the effectiveness of the solution (See **CENTRALIZED VS. DECENTRALIZED SYSTEMS**).

How I use it: I use this concept to identify changes to the variance. This informs both the implied context of the solution and how the context may shift after implementing the solution.

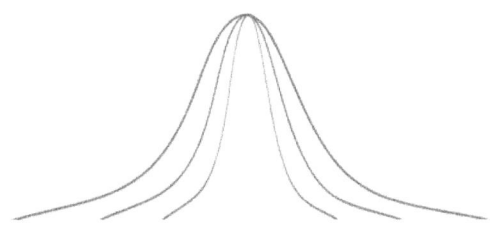

Changing the <u>Average</u>   Changing the <u>Variance</u>

Variance Spectrum: Innovation vs. Risk

Innovation and risk are the two extremes on the spectrum of variance management. Negative consequences are considered risky while positive consequences give organizations the competitive edge. This creates a natural tension between the right mix of innovative pursuits and risk tolerances.

Electric utilities have mitigated risk so well that in the U.S. an average person will only experience one hour of downtime once per year, for an uptime rating of 99.8%. This is even more impressive considering that the electric grid is a 2,500 x 1,500 *square mile man-made machine*, spanning from the coal mine, gas well, solar panel, or wind turbine to the wall socket. It passes through dozens of companies, regulatory bodies, and financial entities. Yet for their successes, they are also blamed for stifling sector innovation.

Technology startups are classic examples of innovation, yet 50% of companies fail to make it past their fifth year. The tradeoff for the innovative mindset is an acceptance of higher risks.

What it's good for: This model depicts innovation management and risk management as two ends of the same spectrum. Techniques for managing risk can be applied to innovation and vice versa.

How I use it: I use this principle to understand the goals of a solution. Being innovative implies pursuing strategies to increase variance. Managing risk implies pursuing strategies to decrease variance.

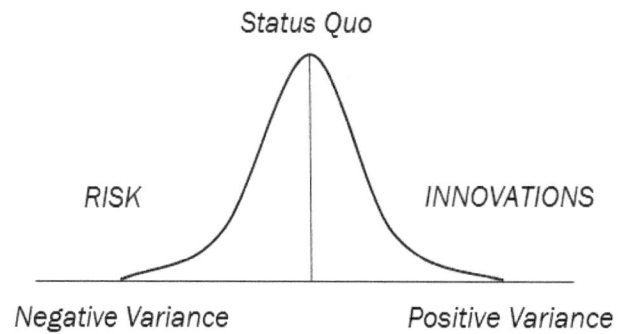

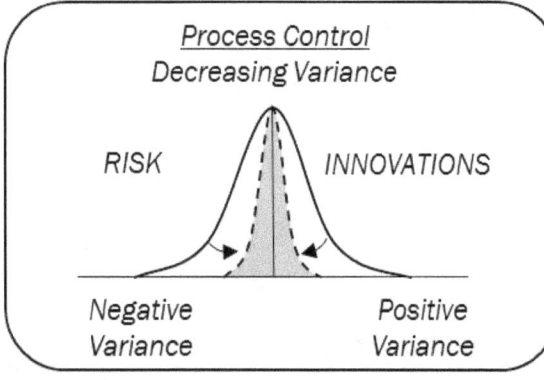

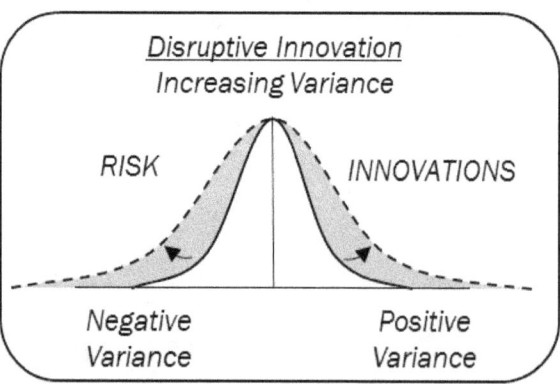

Centralized vs. Decentralized Systems

The properties at the two ends of the **VARIANCE SPECTRUM**: Innovation vs. Riskhelp explain the tension between *centralized* and *decentralized* systems. A *centralized* system reduces variance while a *decentralized* system increases variance.

Key to this tension is that centralized systems are cheaper to operate while decentralized systems are cheaper to implement. Solutions tend to swing between them over time. For instance, data management has evolved from mainframes (centralized data) to personal computers (decentralized data) to cloud solutions (centralized data).

What it's good for: This demonstrates that some combination of properties is not possible to achieve (i.e., a robust and centralized system).

How I use it: I use this to reveal and clarify potential conflicts in the outcomes being optimized. It reduces conflicts within strategies and produces clearer outcomes.

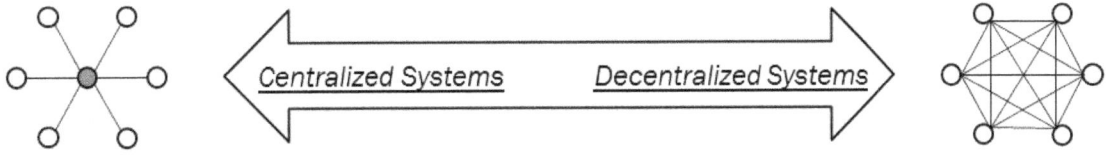

- Efficient Systems
- Few network connections
- Lower variance (process control)
- Fragile
- *Lower cost to operate*
- Higher costs to implement

- Individual Processes
- Many network connections
- Higher variance (intersecting ideas)
- Robust
- Higher cost to operate
- *Lower cost to implement*

Part 2: Business Frameworks

Energy Leadership

Tame problems require commanders.

Complicated problems require experts.

Wicked problems require leaders.

Energy is a classic wicked problem and requires strong leaders who can navigate the complexities of a socio-techno-economic nexus.

This section presents leadership frameworks to help approach the wicked problem that is energy.

The Chief Utility Officer

A Chief Utility Officer is a newer C-suite role responsible for managing a company's utility resource strategy. The position is analogous to the Chief Information Officer when the information technologies (IT) sector underwent dramatic changes in the 1970s. Digital assets are no longer considered a commodity. They are to be used for competitive advantage.

The energy sector faces the same disruptions as energy is no longer just a commodity. Energy responsibilities have expanded from just paying bills to buying solar panels, managing environmental health and safety, and leasing LEED®-rated buildings. Some consumers are differentiating their purchases based on the environmental impact of the product. Companies are improving their resilience and robustness through de-carbonization initiatives. Others are increasing resource productivity to improve profitability.

What it's good for: This model informs the roles and responsibilities for the future of energy and utility resource management.

How I use it: I use it to help assess the maturity of an organization's utility management leadership capabilities. Bringing the responsibility together helps increase visibility and opacity to decisions.

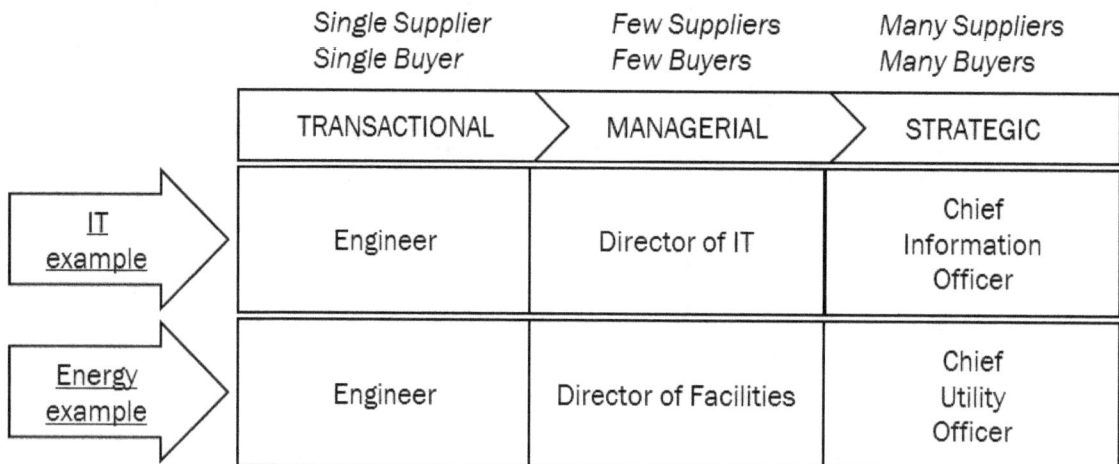

Reference:

J. Jia, *Companies that don't manage utilities strategically are throwing away money*, Harvard Business Review Online, 2016

Seven Principle of Utility Resource Management

These are the best practices gathered through observation of leading companies and their approach to utility management. Responsibility and budget control of utilities needs to be centralized, while planning, implementation and engagement call for multidisciplinary perspectives from throughout the organization.

To help focus the plan on business goals, leading companies create mission / vision statements for their utility resource plan. This helps align stakeholders on the program outcomes and informs tracking for KPIs.

What it's good for: This model shows the different processes and functions the CUO needs to manage and maintain.

How I use it: I use this to evaluate an organization's functional capabilities. Typically, the functions are spread across an organization. Improving organizational effectiveness requires knowing where and how these tasks are accomplished.

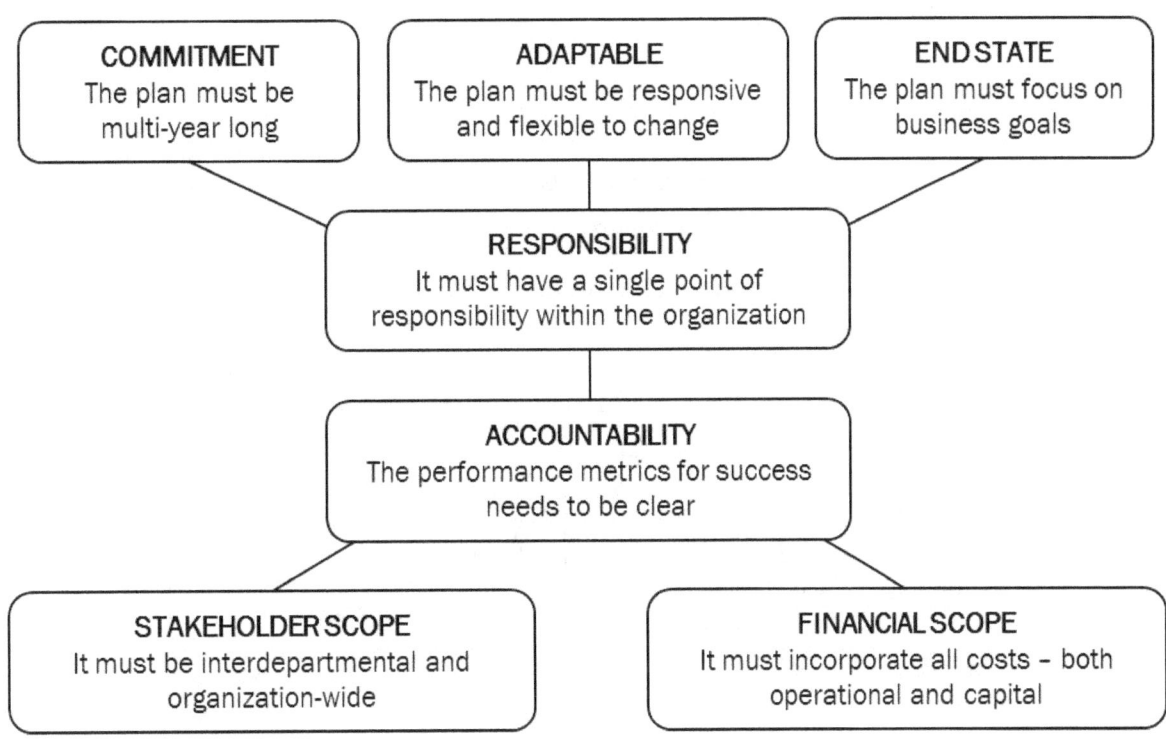

Reference:

The seven steps to utility money management. (2014) Distributed Energy Management www.de-mgmt.com

The Science of Muddling Through

Muddling Through is an empirical observation made on how individuals make decisions with very little information. In an ideal world, leaders have a comprehensive set of data with analyses of every possible outcome to determine the best decision/s. In reality, it is hard and inefficient to gather information on all scenarios, especially to the satisfaction of **THE WICKED PROBLEM**.

Instead, leaders can be effective by making incremental decisions based on available data. The decisions need to move closer to an overarching goal set by the organization. At each step, the stakeholders can re-examine the results, gather new information, and make a new decision or make course corrections.

What it's good for: This process for incremental change can accumulate into massive shifts. It's also a good reminder that in **WICKED PROBLEMS**, picking "no action" is an active choice. Therefore, inaction will have its own benefits and consequences.

How I use it: I use this principle to have the courage to make decisions with limited information. The less information I have, the more mindful I am to seek out new information so that I can continue to make path corrections.

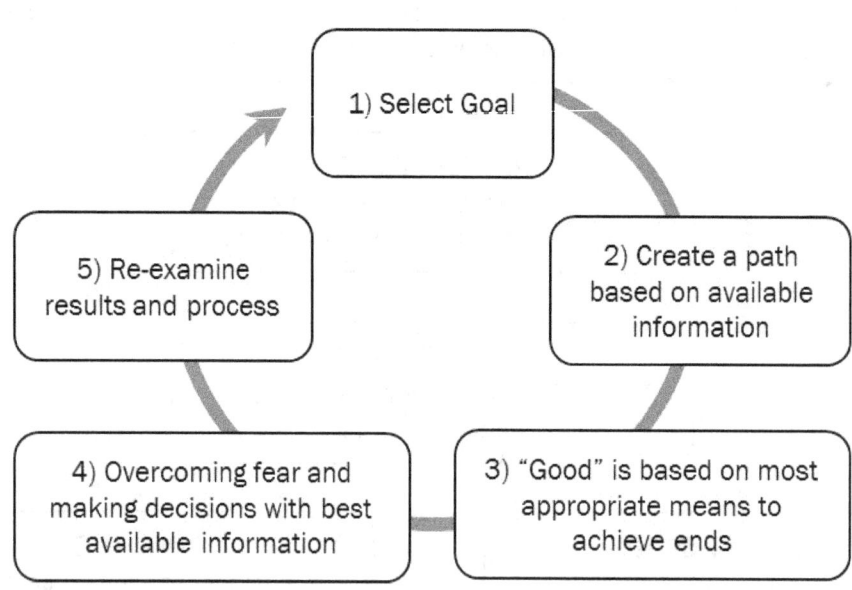

Reference:

Lindblom, CE. (1959), *The science of 'muddling through'*. Public Administration Review, **19**, pp. 79–88

Responsibility Assignment Matrix

A responsibility assignment matrix describes the roles and responsibilities of a team. It is especially useful in complex teams spanning across functions and departments. RACI stands for *Responsible, Accountable, Consulted,* and *Informed.* A team can have only one person accountable for the outcomes and can have many people in the other categories.

A popular alternative is RAPID®, developed by Bain & Company. This one clarifies roles in the decision, not just the role on the team.

- *Recommend* – Gathers information and proposes a course of action.
- *Agree* – People in the formal approval process. Not always required.
- *Perform* – People who are executing or implementing the decision once a decision is made.
- *Input* – An advisory role that provides information to the Recommender and decider.
- *Decide* – Only one per team, the one who is held accountable for the final decision

What it's good for: Clarifying roles and responsibilities of a team

How I use it: Many of my teams are cross-functional and geographically disperse. I like to use RAPID® or RACI to help team members stay aligned and be productive.

R – Recommend
A – Agree
P – Perform
I – Input
D – Decide

Team Member	R	A	P	I	D
1)					
2)					
3)					
4)					
5)					
etc.					

Strategy Frameworks

Businesses adopt strategies to help achieve short-term and long-term goals. Leaders can use strategy frameworks as tools to help analyze the situation, develop plans, and implement actions to reach the desired outcomes.

Since business strategy is contextual, these tools analyze internal, external, micro- and macro-factors for decision support.

These frameworks give the leaders a lay of the land.

Business Model Canvas

The Business Model Canvas is a template that can be used to analyze the strategy and value proposition of a company, division, or product line. Its format helps with the visualization of the knowns and unknowns.

The canvas consists of four parts:

- *Value proposition* – states why a customer should buy the product.
- *Key partners, key activities,* and *key resources* – describes the company infrastructure.
- *Customer relationships, customer segments,* and *channels* – are about the customers.
- *Cost structure* and *revenue stream* – encompasses the financing mechanisms.

What it's good for: The model is good for understanding the major components of a business or a product line. It helps cover the bases when analyzing a new execution strategy or understanding a business model.

How I use it: I use this to treat the "company-as-the-product". Investors buy companies and these are the components they care about when making a purchase. When using this framework, it frequently becomes apparent that some boxes tend to be more fleshed out than others. This helps me spend time appropriately analyzing the whole business.

Key Partners	Key Activities	Value Proposition	Customer Relationships	Customer Segments
	Key Resources		Channels	
Cost Structure			Revenue Stream	

Reference:

Osterwalder A., et. al., (2010) *Business model generation*, self published, https://strategyzer.com/

4 P's of the Marketing Mix

The Marketing Mix is a tool that a company can use to meet their marketing goals for a product or service. Since its inception, there have been many variations – including expanding the framework to up to 8 P's. Consumer-driven models, such as the 4 C's or the 7 C's have been developed as well.

- *Product* – the product itself needs to satisfy the customer's needs and wants.
- *Price* – the price needs to reflect the perceived value and support the larger business model.
- *Place* – where a customer gains access to the product. This could be bricks & mortar location or online.
- *Promotion* – communicating to the customer, such as advertisements or direct marketing.

What it's good for: This framework helps a company consider factors in their marketing strategy. The information gathered must support the larger vision of the organization. These 4 P's can also help determine the right KPI's for the marketing efforts.

How I use it: I use it to cover my bases in analyzing or creating a marketing strategy.

5 C's of Situational Analysis

Marketing strategies succeed if the plan takes into consideration internal and external influences. The 5 C's is a review of how a business is positioned in the market. It analyzes both macro- and micro-environmental factors.

- *Company* – The company's ability to deliver on a promise. This includes the financial strength (business model) as well as the product's value proposition and performance record.
- *Competitors* – The competitor's ability to deliver on the same or similar promise.
- *Collaborators* – The collaborators are those that enable the company to gain more business opportunities. This could be distributors, suppliers, partners, etc.
- *Customers* – The customer's shifting needs and requirements. This could be due to changing market size, customer motivation, how you're reaching them, etc.
- *Context* (or *climate*) – The larger business, political and social context. Decisions may be affected by political, economic, social and technology (PEST) factors.

What it's good for: This builds on product marketing strategy to also consider the market positioning of the company. A correct positioning can increase competitiveness.

How I use it: I use this to cover my bases in the market position and company strategy to improve market share.

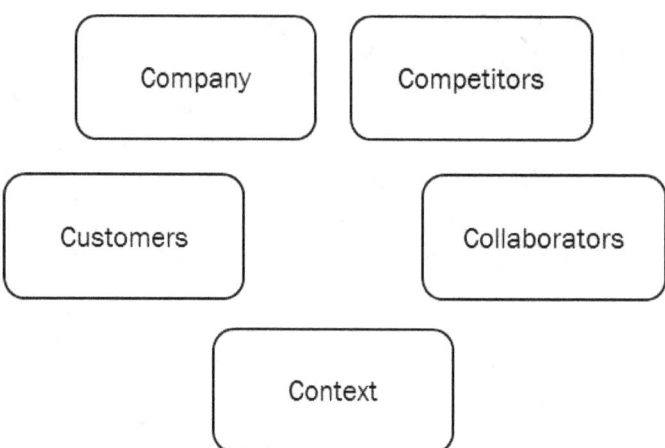

Porter's Five Forces for Industry Analysis

Porter's five forces were developed to understand the level of competition in an industry. By understanding these dynamics, a company can determine their competitive advantage.

- *Suppliers* and *Buyers* have bargaining power that can squeeze the profit margins. Suppliers can raise the prices of raw materials while buyers might pick between many producers.
- *New Entrants* and *Substitutions* can threaten the market position with new products. Fast-growing markets will attract new entrants trying to establish themselves. Customers may also find substitutes that also meet their needs, such as using Lyft, Uber or other car-sharing applications instead of buying a car.
- *Industry Rivals* are also innovating to gain market share of the same market. They will be developing their own strategies and execution plans.

What it's good for: An analysis of the competitive forces in an industry. It demonstrates where threats may come from and how an organization might mitigate these threats.

How I use it: I use this to cover my bases in understanding an industry's dynamics.

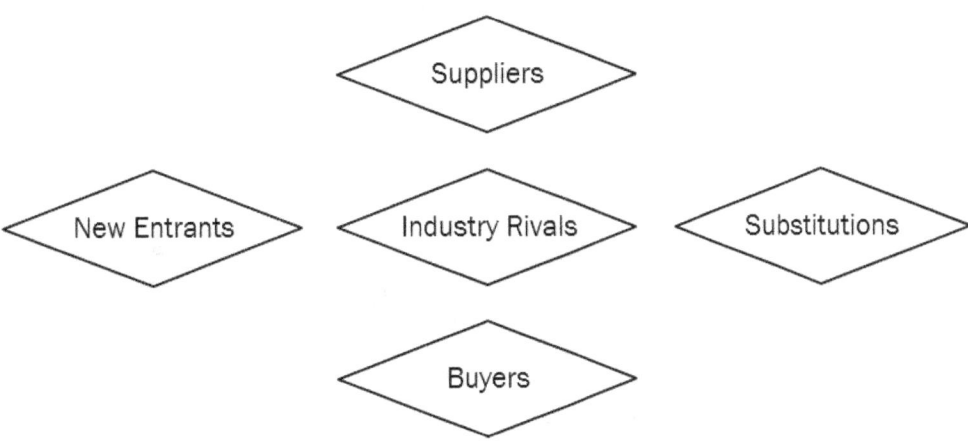

Reference:
Porter, M.E. (1979) *How competitive forces shape strategy*, Harvard Business Review **57** 137-145

Diffusion of Innovation

Innovations are rarely overnight successes. Rather, the theory of the diffusion of innovation explain how ideas are adopted over time. The drivers of adoption are the innovation itself, communication channels, time, and the social system. The model can be used to describe the adoption of a technical innovation or to describe the acceptance of change management in an organization.

The cumulative number of adopters creates an "S" curve, so called because of its shape. If the adoption rate is very high, one is still acquiring the *early* and *late majorities*. If adoption rates slow down, one is probably near market saturation.

What it's good for: The position on the innovation curve informs what strategy to pursue for further adoption. Marketing to *early adopters* is very different than customer acquisition of the *laggards*.

How I use it: I use this to understand what adoption strategy to implement, what type of team to form and what expectations to set for the outcome.

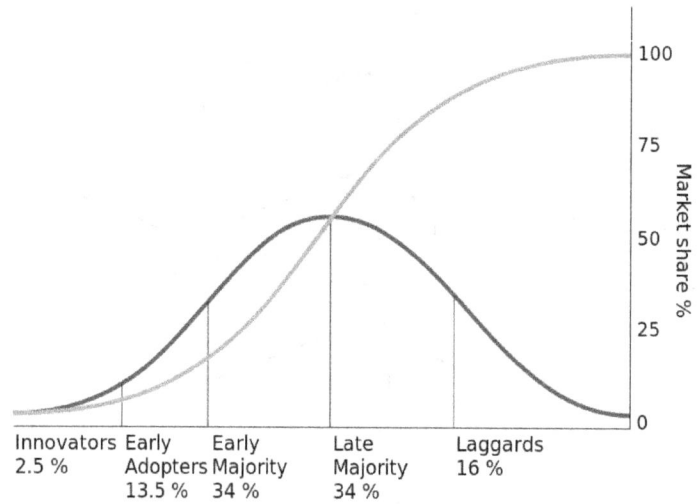

Reference:

Rogers, E. (2003). *Diffusion of innovations*, 5th Edition. Simon and Schuster

Process Frameworks

Process frameworks are a set of tools that leaders use to implement actions. Formally, the field of Business Process Management (BPM) helps companies become more effective.

The frameworks picked for this section are examples of process frameworks. They can be used to achieve specific outcomes, such as team management or ideal situation analysis.

Ideal Situation Analysis

Ideal Situation Analysis helps create priorities that can be used to evaluate actions, plans, and strategies. The four-step process is:

- **Step 1**: Write down the properties of the worst-case scenario of what could happen.
  Ex: Prospective client drags a purchasing decision for over a year.
- **Step 2**: Write down the properties of the best-case scenario of what could happen.
  Ex: Prospective client needs a solution tomorrow.
- **Step 3**: Write down up to five properties that avoid the worst case and indicate best-case
  Ex: Ideal client is one that has budget to solve their critical problems today.
- **Step 4**: Rate each possible action or scenario from -5 to 5 against each of the properties.
  Avoid using 0's as no action should have a neutral outcome. This prioritizes the actions into a plan.

What it's good for: The process can be applied to any situations where a leader needs to understand the ideal properties of a goal. It defines the boundary conditions of the best and worst before synthesizing the ideal.

How I use it: I've most frequently used this in sales to create ideal client profiles. Recently, I've used it to evaluate potential investors and product development priorities.

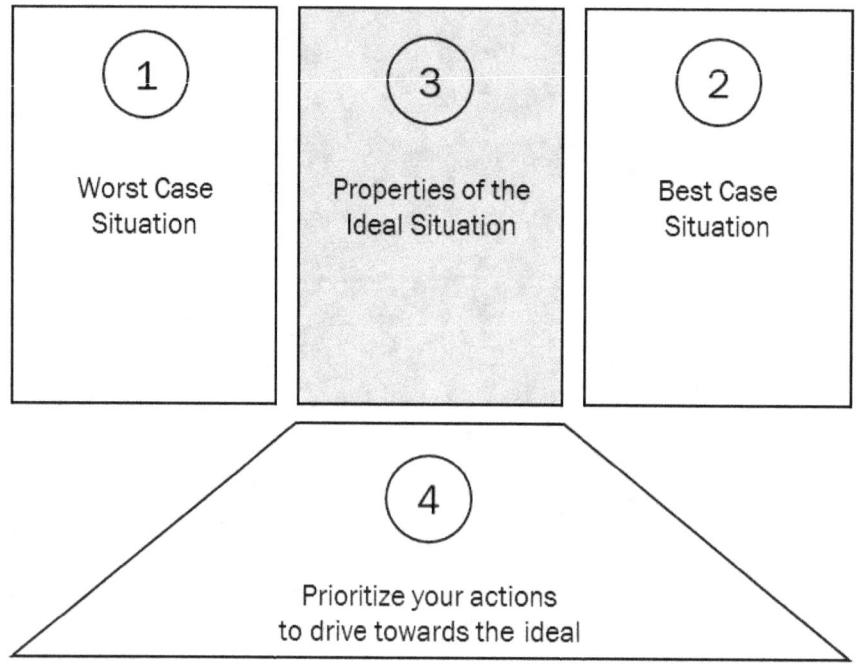

Financial Risk Management

Risk Management is a field that identifies and quantifies the effect of uncertainty. Insurance is a financial form of risk management to hedge against a future loss.

Reactively, insurance is used to help with recovery from a negative event – car crash, heart attack surgery, or theft. It *transfers* the responsibility of the risk to a cleanup or recovery effort. Proactively, insurance can incentivize eliminating the root cause of the risk – driving carefully, exercising daily, or installing a security system. Proactive risk management not only reduces the financial loss, it also reduces the downtime, staff time to manage the issue, and creates a more resilient organization.

What it's good for: These frameworks help a leader understand how they are approaching risk mitigation strategies.

How I use it: When given a choice, I pick options that are proactive in risk mitigation rather than reactive in risk transfer.

Value **DESTRUCTION** in the insurance industry pays people to clean up their messes.
- Cleanup of asbestos in a building.
- Remediation of a superfund site.

Value **CREATION** in the insurance industry encourages good behaviors.
- Reduced car insurance premiums for teens with high GPA.
- Prohibit skydiving from life insurance policies.

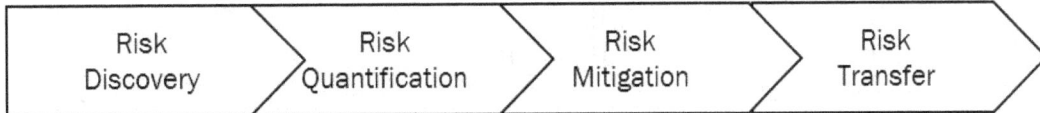

:

Reference:
The global state of sustainable insurance. (2009) United Nations Environment Programme Finance Initiative

Scrum Process

Agile is a set of principles and practices for adaptive project development. Scrum is an Agile framework for iterative and incremental development. Scrum assumes that unknowns and challenges will reveal themselves during the development of any project. Therefore, the method focuses the ability to respond to emergent requirements.

Some teams create, prioritize, and break down a project into the following components:

- *Epic* – Major goals or arcs (i.e., acquire 100 new clients)
- *Story* – Smaller goals distilled from the epic (i.e., run an advertising campaign to reach 1,000 prospects)
- *Prioritized Tasks* – Tasks that take no more than 4 hours (i.e., draft the newsletter to send)
- *Sprint Backlog* – Tasks assigned to be completed during a sprint (see KANBAN)
- *2-Week Sprint* – The set of tasks to be completed in the next two weeks
- *24-Cycle Short* – Daily updates to track progress
- *New Functionality* – Meeting the goals of a story

What it's good for: Keeping a team on track and working towards often fast changing goals.

How I use it: I use this to manage major projects and to make sure I'm on track for quarterly or annual goals.

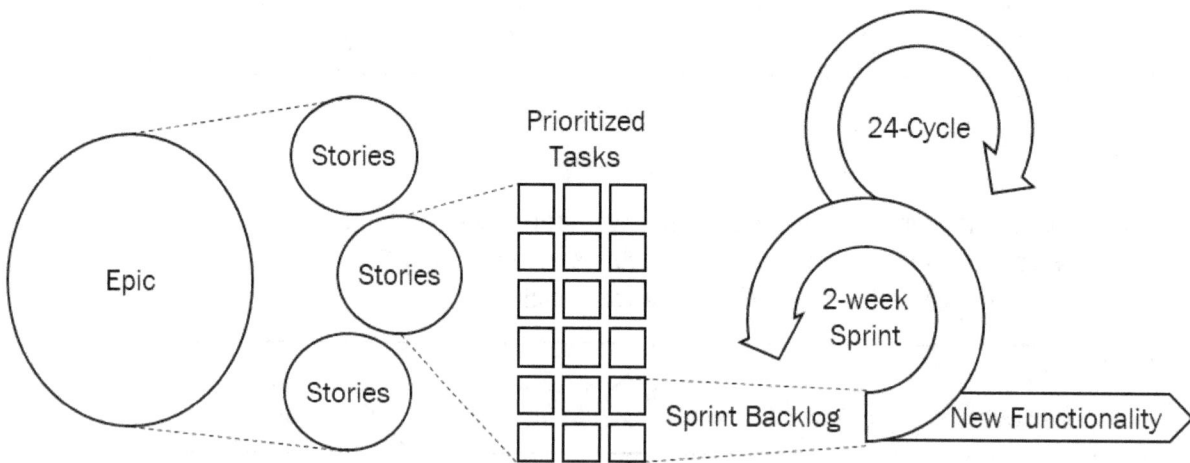

Kanban Process

The Kanban Process is a method of achieving continuous delivery at a high level of efficiency. Key among it is a workflow visualization method, establishing an upper limit to the work in process, and a pull methodology of replenishing tasks. Key metrics is lead time and cycle time of the process components. Developed to manage inventory, this can also be used to manage tasks and projects.

- The visualization method shows where inventory or tasks are located in the process. As tasks get completed, cards are physically moved through the process.
- In limiting the work in process, managers can encourage finishing of projects at hand instead of starting more tasks. This creates more capacity in the system for new work.
- The pull methodology minimizes bottlenecks in the process. Tasks are requested and completed when resources become available.

What it's good for: It keeps a team's deliverables clear, transparent, and accountable to each other.

How I use it: I use this process to manage my own personal to do list as well as the activities of my teams.

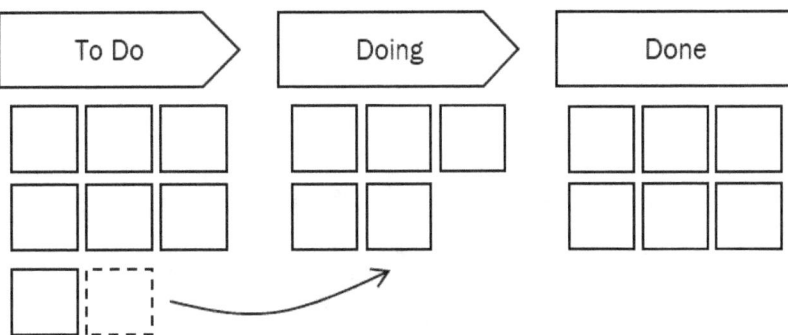

Communication Frameworks

Communicating ideas is just as important as developing them in the first place. Solutions are only as effective as their adoption.

These frameworks are generic templates that can be adopted for any story arc. They help get the message across.

The message being delivered can be in person, in a meeting, or in writing.

The Message House

The Message House is an internal document that is the foundation to help companies stay on message when communicating. It is a living document that gets revisited and updated based on need.

Structurally, the Message House consists of an overarching umbrella statement, four core messages, and each core messages contains four supporting statements. This limits the Message House to at most 17 statements, a difficult exercise for any organization. The result is a set of themes, keywords and concepts that helps the company stay on point when communicating internally and externally.

What it's good for: Out of the Message House, a leader can draft the mission and vision statements, elevator pitch, marketing collateral, website, job descriptions, blog entries and virtually any other written or oral communications.

How I use it: Before I start any new initiative, I always write a first draft using the Message House. It helps me clarify my ideas while drafting any other document. I usually expect two years, if not more, of iterations before I'm satisfied with a Message House.

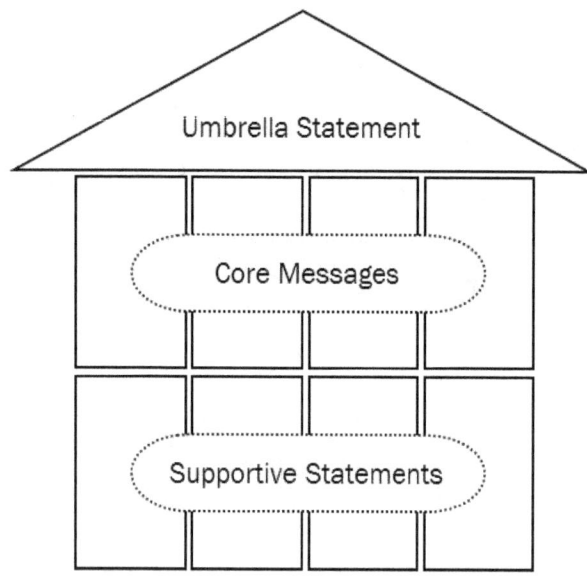

Umbrella Statement

- *Core Message #1*
  - *Supportive statement 1*
  - *Supportive statement 2*
  - *Supportive statement 3*
  - *Supportive statement 4*
- *Core Message #2*
- *Core Message #3*
- *Core Message #4*

For More Information:
http://www.messagehouse.org

The 6-Sentence Story

People are attracted to stories. This 6-Sentence Story is an outline that encompasses the basics of any plot, whether only a paragraph long or the entirety of Tolkien's epics.

There are several ways to extend the structure. *Because of that* can be repeated ad infinitum. The entire structure can also be nested as mini-stories inside a larger story arc. An example of that in fiction is when a character tells a story through a flashback.

What it's good for: Structuring content into this format gives it a plot arc that helps engage the reader or audience. It organizes the information to build up to a conclusion. It also helps pace the story evenly so one spends the right amount of time on each topic.

How I use it: I use this framework to create outlines for an article or presentation. Once I'm satisfied with the story structure, I'll modify each sentence into the opening of each paragraph or the first slide of each section.

Once upon a time, _____.

Every day, _____.

Until one day, _____.

Because of that, _____.

Because of that, _____.

And ever since then, _____.

Here's an example storyline that helped me prepare a lecture on Carbon Tax Policies:

Once upon a time,	Societies wanted to control the long-term negative risk of releasing CO_2.
Every day,	Businesses were concerned that a new tax would hurt the economy.
Until one day,	Long-term climate risks began affecting short-term profits.
Because of that,	Businesses started implementing internal carbon taxes as a risk-mitigation strategy.
Because of that,	Policy designers borrowed best-practices of other public benefit tax policies.
And ever since then,	Government and businesses designed an *effective* tax that achieved policy goals while growing the economy.

Chasm Statement

A chasm statement is an elevator pitch framework. Geoffrey Moore proposed it in his book, *Crossing the Chasm*. It can be used to bridge the divide between *innovators* and the *early majority* in the **DIFFUSION OF INNOVATION** model. Frequently, the general public can feel confused by a new innovation because they don't know how to relate to it yet. Henry Ford's automobile was a horseless carriage that did not require oats nor left behind manure. Thomas Edison's lightbulb was a candle that didn't burn down your house.

What it's good for: This messaging framework helps make an innovation feel familiar. When trying to market a new product for the first time, it creates the first draft of a pitch to be given to the *innovators*. When used for an existing and nascent product, it helps explain to the *early majority* why the *innovators* adopted it.

How I use it: I use it as a first-pass pitch when trying to test the value proposition of an innovation.

For _____,
(target customers)

who are dissatisfied with _____,
(the current market alternative)

our product is a _____,
(new product category)

that provides _____,
(key problem-solving capability)

unlike _____,
(the product alternative)

our product _____.
(describe the key product features)

Reference:

Moore, GA., (2014) *Crossing the Chasm 3rd Ed.* Collins Business Essentials

Executive Summary / Pitch / Business Plan

An executive summary, pitch deck, and business plan all follow the same structure. They differ in their purpose, format, and length. A pitch is usually 10-15 slides, an executive summary is 1-page while a business plan can vary from 10-25 pages or longer. Both the pitch and executive summary are introductions to a business, while the plan is more comprehensive with execution detail and market analysis.

A quick search online will reveal many variations of this template, both in terms of the section titles as well as the order. Regardless of the template, the content should come from the BUSINESS MODEL CANVAS.

What it's good for: The outline helps a leader cover their bases when pitching the "company-as-the-product" to an investor.

How I use it: In addition to pitching, I use this outline to reveal weaknesses and unknowns in my business. I then update the operating plan with actions to address the weakness and investigate the unknowns.

```
Opportunity / value proposition

Problem

Solution

Target market

Traction / validation

Go-to-Market strategy

Competition

Revenue model

Team

Financials

Exit plan / recent exits

Ask / use of funds
```

Running Meetings with the Circle Framework

When school is in session at the MBA program where I teach, the day starts with the community gathering for Circle. These sessions consist of sharing of joys and worries, discussions of critical issues, and end with uplifting hopes for the future. Regardless of the seriousness of what was discussed, I always leave feeling energized. Circle follows this general format:

- *Appreciations* – sets the tone for a positive meeting by appreciate individuals and groups.
- *New Information* – announcements to the community and other communications of facts.
- *Puzzles* – quandaries that the speaker may not quite know how to phrase. This is a way to query the community for wisdom.
- *Problems with Solutions* – any problem presented needs to be accompanied with a proposed solution. Responses also need to be accompanied with alternative solutions.
- *Hopes and Dreams* – synthesizing the content of the meeting with what the future holds.

What it's good for: Circle creates an ethos of appreciation and avoids a culture of complaints for the community. This method can manage meetings with as many as 70-100 individuals, in a respectful manner, where everyone feels heard, and advances the community goals.

How I use it: I use this model when running business meetings. *Appreciations* become Introductions. *New Information* is a form of Officer Reports. *Puzzles* can be used to generate a list of Topics for Discussion and *problems with solutions* are the facilitated Discussions themselves. *Hopes and dreams* become Comments for the Good of the Order.

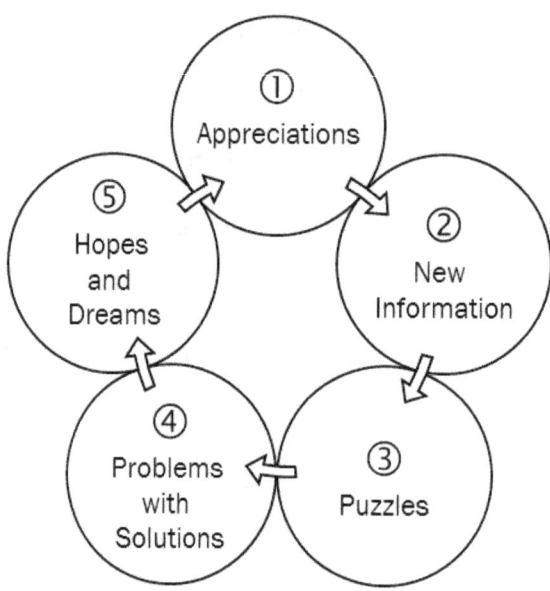

Crowdsourcing Puzzles: I Like, I Wish, I Wonder

Puzzles create a mental framework that enables teams to find the root cause instead of treating the symptom. A *Problem with Solution* can usually be stated out of the puzzles (see RUNNING MEETINGS WITH THE CIRCLE FRAMEWORK).

One method for creating puzzles is the *I like, I wish, I wonder* process.

I like... roots the puzzle in something that already happens today.

I wish... creates the space of where an improvement might be.

I wonder... frames a pathway for exploration.

What it's good for: This is a way to generate consensus of problem statements while avoiding attacking a person or process.

An example: *I like* the central location of my desk. *I wish* there wasn't a draft. *I wonder* if I can be engaged without feeling cold. Solutions to this problem could be a space heater to warm the individual, shifting the desk away from a vent, or putting a plant to block a draft. Any innovative solution that helps the person stay warm would solve this problem.

How I use it: I use this as a team exercise to generate consensus for problem statements. This creates space to spur innovations.

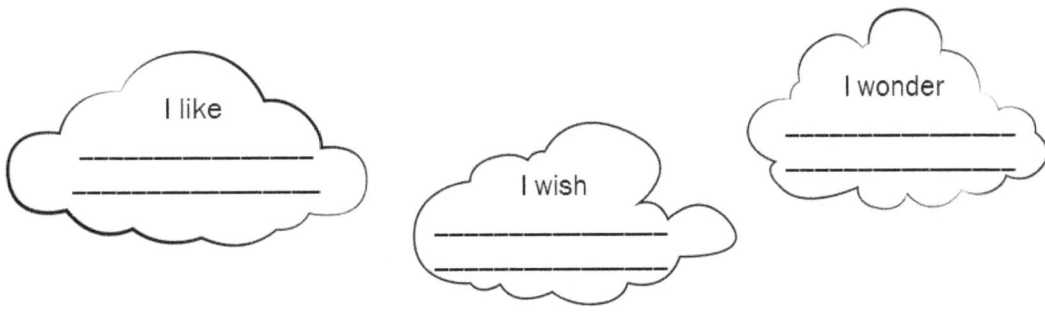

Epilogue

This project was borne out of a request to compile a list of all the frameworks from my energy leadership class into one reference book.

Leadership is a craft and frameworks are its tools. Leaders can hone their skills by applying these tools to situations and becoming familiar with the outcomes. Historical stories are great case studies to learn from other people's experiences.

One challenge I faced was to present the framework in a logical order. As I experimented with different groupings, new connections between frameworks emerged.

A few of the Carbon Management Frameworks revealed themselves as logical combinations of the energy and financial literacy frameworks.

This became an example of innovating-in-action: combining ideas from two different sectors to create new ideas.

I hope the reader will collect their own frameworks for their own development. This book is a good start; however, this is not an exhaustive list. Probably many frameworks are missing. If you tweet me your favorite framework, I may include it in a future edition!

Thank you for reading.

Jimmy Y. Jia
@jimmyYjia

NOTES: